SUMMARY

Entrepreneurship means different things to different people – there is no one universally accepted definition. Many people think that anyone in business is an entrepreneur; unfortunately, this is not the case. Many businesses are not entrepreneurial.

Entrepreneurial businesses are founded upon exceptional business opportunities, innovative products and/or services that help to differentiate them in the market, and extraordinary entrepreneurial teams who know how to grow the business and play the entrepreneurial game. These businesses exhibit rapid growth and, in the process, generate wealth for their owners and their communities and create employment.

Entrepreneurship is relevant in both business and social contexts. In a business context, entrepreneurs establish new businesses and develop existing businesses. Entrepreneurs also can be involved in larger public and private sector organisations where they assume the role of corporate entrepreneurs ("intrapreneurs") while working as employees. In this environment, they help to identify and develop business opportunities for their employers.

In a social context, entrepreneurial principles are just as relevant in helping social entrepreneurs develop their not-for-profit entities providing them with a basis of generating funds from non-traditional sources. Social entrepreneurs are also involved in developing socially disadvantaged communities, helping unemployed individuals in those communities develop businesses that can form the basis of employment and revenue generation while, at the same time, helping them to feel empowered and socially included.

These and other topics will be discussed in this book including what characterises exceptional business opportunities, characteristics of winning entrepreneurial teams, can we differentiate entrepreneurs from non-entrepreneurs, and what are the financing strategies that entrepreneurs use to grow their entrepreneurial pie (increase the value of their businesses).

How to be an Entrepreneur

Many of us want to become entrepreneurs. Starting your own business is one of the biggest dreams of our times. But how do you get to be an entrepreneur?

HOW TO BE AN ENTREPRENEUR

BY ANSUMAN SAHOO

Most of the advice focuses on the practicalities: writing a business plan, raising money, finding staff, marketing and PR. We'll go down a different route. In our eyes at the heart of successful entrepreneurship lies something oddly more abstract: an accurate insight into the causes of human unhappiness.

To be an entrepreneur means, essentially, to become an expert in the things that make life difficult for people. That's because every properly ambitious business is in some way trying to fix things for other people. And the bigger and more original what you're trying to fix happens to be, the more successful your business can be. Because consumer society is now well developed, it may be easy to think that all the big problems out there already have thousands of fixes anyway. Think of all those car companies, or pizza outlets, or news websites. We surely have enough of everything. What could we possibly add to what's already out there?

But to get a sense of the vast opportunities that still remain in capitalism all you need to do is ask yourself: where and in what areas you're unhappy in the course of an average day? Every unhappiness is really a new business waiting to be born. Your frustrations are a nearly inexhaustible source of raw materials out of which the businesses of the future can be built.

So, while there may already be plenty of breakfast cereals, and t-shirts, and cell phones, and cab rides for sale, there's so much more than frustrates and depresses us: think of how difficult it is to get on with one's partner, educate children, cope with anxiety, discover what you want to do with your life, find a nice place to live, calm down in the evening. One could go on and on. Our griefs and irritations are endless, thankfully for the budding entrepreneurs.

The biggest first step to take towards entrepreneurship is, therefore, to learn to study your own unhappiness and what might possibly heal it for you and others. When profits decline in businesses it's really the result of too many people throwing themselves at trying to fix the same area because they can't think of anything more innovative to do rather than start a new airline, mobile phone company, or supermarket chain. And by contrast, healthy profits are a reward for understanding and mastering an area of human distress ahead of anyone else. Of course, ideas aren't enough on their own; you need to take care of practicalities and money but they won't help you if your original psychological insight into human unhappiness isn't sound. And by the same token, if your insight into what makes people unhappy is razor-sharp, and your solutions bold, then however difficult the journey, your business will stand a high chance of making money and benefiting humanity too.

An Idea or a Wish? What Do You Have?

What do you need to succeed as a start-up or a business?

The answer is simple and straightforward.

You should make the right decisions at the right moments, but the problem is, you won't know whether your choices are right or wrong until you put them to work and see the results.

But there is one thing you can do, which is avoiding the mistakes entrepreneurs usually make at the critical junctures of building a start-up—ideation, validation, building an MVP, and getting your customers.

That's what we are going to address in this and the following emails, because when you know the mistakes you should avoid, you can probably be on the right track.

Let's start with the mistakes of the ideation stage.

Picking the right idea for your start-up is challenging and critical for your success. A right product idea can put you on the fast track to success, while a wrong idea can set you back, costing you time, effort, and money.

People choose their start-up idea in different ways. That's where a lot of entrepreneurs make their first mistake.

It's working for someone else

Often people choose an idea just because it's working for someone else. That's a mistake.

Each one of us is different. Who we are and what we can do differ?

Because something works for someone doesn't mean you can also do it and produce similar results. You could pull it off or even do it better than the other, and it is also possible that you'll fail because you lack what is required to execute the idea.

The other guy is doing it because he has his own reasons and you don't have those reasons. You are doing it because it's working for him or her. And at the sight of the first trouble, you'll bounce from the idea because you don't know how to handle the situation or how the other guy handled the situation.

Because there is a lot more going on inside than what you see from outside.

It's trending

Do you remember how many started a some-kart business when Flipkart became a unicorn?

A lot.

But do you know how many of them survived?

A lot less.

See, following the trends is an excellent way to pick an idea, but that doesn't guarantee success by default because your success depends on whether or not you are good enough to turn that idea into a working business.

Many of the "karts" failed because people didn't have a clue about running an e-commerce business while the Bansal knew what they were doing.

But that's only one side of the problem.

The other side is that people aren't considering the three main criteria for a successful business idea:

Whether or not they have what it takes to make the idea work;

Whether or not there is a market need for the idea; and

Whether they can sell it or not.

Let me explain.

What it takes to make the idea work

The idea is just the beginning.

There is a long journey between coming up with the idea and turning it into a working product or service, and it takes a lot of work. It takes countless hours of disciplined work as an individual and a team, executing a well-crafted plan toward a well-defined goal.

That's what people don't realize. When they come face-to-face with the workload, they feel overwhelmed and lost.

Whether there is a market need or not

This is probably the biggest mistake any entrepreneur can make and still most make.

Your idea isn't worth a penny if it isn't meeting a market need.

It doesn't matter how innovative or exciting the idea is, it should fulfil a market need or solve a market problem.

Whether you can sell it or not

You might have the best idea or product, but if you can't sell it to your target market, which is, if your target market isn't willing to pay for it, none of it matters.

People will be willing to pay for a solution or an idea only if it benefits them somehow and makes their lives better—not for the features or how fantastic the idea is.

People want to get better and quicker results in doing simpler things. If your idea or product is not doing that, you can't sell it. If your product produces better and faster results but is complex to use, you can't sell it and so on.

But in the ideation phase, people don't consider it, and most entrepreneurs start thinking about the sales part after they have invested a lot in building the product or solution only to face the bitter fact that no one is willing to pay for it.

And that's why often ideas are just wishes and nothing more.

For example:

I'll start a restaurant or any offline business or will start consulting, or a service-based business or will build a SAAS product or an app or a website or something else.

These aren't ideas but your wishes, things you want to do. But just because you want to do something, it doesn't mean you can do it or you'll succeed in doing it, or it'll work out well and make you money.

I call it a wish because of the pure nature of those statements.

Let me take the restaurant example and explain it.

I'll start a restaurant.

I call it a wish, not an idea, because it's just a statement. There's no logic or reason behind the statement, nor does it explain how and why you consider the idea a good one or a workable one.

You could have picked the idea because of the reasons we've discussed so far.

And you probably haven't considered whether there is a market need or not, whether you have the skills to start and manage a restaurant business, or whether people will buy from you or not.

I've seen a lot of restaurants pop up now and then fade away in six months or so, probably because they didn't think it through.

But if you turn the statement into something like this.

I'm going to start a restaurant because people in this area don't have access to x cuisine, have to drive y km for such a restaurant, or are from the y location and love the cuisine. Also, people in the surrounding area with a radius of around 5 km too prefer this cuisine and can be served via delivery platforms.

Or

I'm going to start a restaurant because I've seen people are waiting in front of restaurants x and y, which have limited seating capacity, while their customers spend a long time on the meals. If I provide similar features and facilities, I could convert those who couldn't get a table as my customers.

It is still not perfect enough reason to start a restaurant, but it transforms the wish into an idea because you've thought it through a bit.

It's a good start, and you might even succeed if you execute it right.

Now it's your turn.

What do you have? An idea or a wish?

How a leader should lead

During the starting of my career, I was working in an IT company. In the beginning, they had a small group. There weren't a lot of people in the company. There was a family vibe there and it was good. They were providing a very good service and it was always on time. Everything seemed to be fine, as they were growing and they had different visions and ideas for the future. Then the CEO decided to spend less on employees and then everything turned into shit. They faced difficulties in getting back to their clients. They weren't even delivering on what they promised and I looked at that and I would say the biggest problem they had was because the CEO lacks leadership skills. The company itself had outgrown the capabilities of the CEO. There are many different forms of leadership styles. One, you could have leaders who are leading by a dictatorship. Meaning it's their way or the highway. They think there is only one way to do something and they don't listen to anybody. It's very much like top to bottom. This is how they do it. They don't listen to anybody. Now it might work in the old days but it doesn't work today, especially when you're working with young people.

The young people want to express themselves right. They want to have space where they could grow. They want to voice out their opinions. As a leader, you have to listen to them. Or have to have some people who are good at managing people. Those people should lead by consense. Meaning, they should wait for everybody. They should wait for everybody to agree on something. Everybody should like their decision. They shouldn't hurt anyone's feelings.

But the problem with that is, nothing gets done by this. It doesn't get done. You're not moving forward because you care way too much about other people's feelings versus the job, what needs to be done. And sometimes a leader got to make a tough decision and you're going to make some decisions that are not popular. That may be your people. And your team doesn't like it. But that's why you are in the leadership position. You get paid the big bucks because you can make those tough decisions. That's your job, not anybody's job. No-one can do that for you.

Leadership style should be actually very simple. It should be managed by persuasion. Meaning you have to find out the goals, the dreams of each member. What do they want? Where do they want to be? Once you understand their personality type, once you understand their goals and dreams, you should put them in the right seat. And sometimes where you think is the right seat may not be the right seat right away. Your job's not to micro-manage. Your job is to create the platform and the environment. So, the employees could flourish and it will give them clear milestones.

So, they hit those milestones and leaders holding them accountable. Done properly, they should hold themselves accountable. That should be the leadership style. You shouldn't believe in micro-managing because as you grow you cannot micro-manage. You cannot be going in there is a control freak trying to "oh, how about this, how about that". You can't control every little thing. If you will then you won't be able to grow. You will not be able to scale if you do it this way. You have to let go. You have to put your ego aside. You should be okay with when it's not done exactly the way you want it to be 100%. But it is done. At least it's done.

The pride of ownership kills a business more than anything else. You're choking your business to death. You're not letting go. You're not trusting people. What you're really saying is you're not trusting yourself as a leader, that's why you don't trust nobody.

So, a leader should have the qualities to trust people, make a tough decision and to listen to people before making any bold move.

Seven principles to get rich

You want to know how to get rich. Rich Dad Poor Dad is the

story of Robert Kiyosaki.

He had two dads one had a Ph.D., while the other had only finished eighth grade. Although both dads are in a significant amount of money. Poor dad always struggled, while rich dad was on his way to becoming one of the richest men in

Hawaii. If you weren't born with rich parents, you can learn from Kiyosaki to become wealthy. You can use the principles in this book.

The first principle is the rich don't work for money. The rich don't trade their time for money. Instead, they acquire assets to make money for them. One of my favourite quotes goes a little something like this. "Most of the time life does not talk to you. It just sorts of pushes you around and each push is life saying wake up." If you want to become wealthy you must know that people's lives are controlled by two emotions, fear and greed. Fear and greed can lead you into life's biggest trap.

The second principle in the book is called financial literacy. If you want to get rich it's not about how much money you make. It's about how much money you keep intelligently to solve problems and produces money. But money without intelligence is money soon gone. This is one of the only rules you'll ever need to know if you want to become rich. A lack of financial knowledge is the number one reason why the rich get richer and the poor get poorer.

The third principle from the book is minding your own business. To sum this principle up, the book is telling you that the rich focus on their assets, while everyone else focuses on their income. Statements to follow this principle you need to build and maintain a strong group of assets. An asset might be a piece of real estate, a website or anything that produces positive cash flow for you every single month.

The fourth principle from the book is the power of corporations. Corporations are one of the biggest secrets of the rich and they serve as a smarter way to play the game of life. The rich used corporations to take advantage of legal tax loopholes and protect their money. If you own a business and make a decent amount of money, you need to consider setting up cooperation to get rich. The book says that you need to train your financial IQ which is comprised of your knowledge across several broad subjects to increase your financial IQ. You must increase your knowledge in the areas of accounting, investing, understanding markets and the law. Accounting is for reading and understanding numbers and investing is for using your money to make more money. Understanding markets is the science of supply and demand and the law is understanding tax laws on how to keep more of your own money. Once again, a corporation is one of the biggest legal tax loopholes used by the rich to make and keep more of their money. Your financial IQ is a synergy of all of these skills and talents combined.

The fifth principle from the book is the rich invent money. This principle can be summed up as the rich see opportunities to invest money. Remember that great opportunities are not seen with your eyes. They are seen with your mind. The single most powerful asset you have in your mind and if trained well, it can create enormous wealth for you. Another important point from the book is in the real world, it is not the smart who get ahead. This means that the bold or risk-takers tend to make the most financial progress even if they're not as smart as others.

The sixth principle from the book says to work to learn. Don't work for money. This means that rich people work to learn and not for job security. If you want to get rich, you should know a little bit about a lot of subjects. One of my favourite quotes is, a job is an acronym for just over broke. It means that focusing only on a job will prevent you from becoming truly wealthy.

The seventh principle of the book is overcoming obstacles. The primary difference between a rich person and a poor person is how they manage fear. Even if you have an excellent financial IQ, there are a few major obstacles that will hold you back from becoming rich. These obstacles are fear cynicism, laziness, bad habits, and arrogance. Some people are so afraid of losing that they lose. Cynicism is the kind of like another word for self-doubt and for many, it's a major obstacle. Laziness is another obstacle that we all struggle with. Bad habits can have the same effect. Stop watching so much Netflix and going out to drink on the weekends. The final obstacle that everyone must face is arrogance. Robert Kiyosaki said, every time I've been arrogant, I've lost money. Because I believed that what I didn't know wasn't important. Don't let arrogance steal your money.

7 Daily habits of self-made millionaires

Everyone has a fantasy to become a millionaire before 30. But most don't able to become millionaire till their thirties. In fact, most are Financially Struggling. At that time, we started thinking, like what mistakes we are doing because of which we aren't getting success. We started searching the reason which makes other people millionaire. Like what are the secrets which make a person millionaire? what are the things which makes an average poor person a millionaire? We all search answer for all these questions. We study this topic for years, and our research tells us that this (era) is the best time to become a millionaire. Because nowadays due to a lot of opportunities, there are more millionaires compare to earlier. Most of the millionaires have some specific qualities, habits and behaviour which helps them to become a millionaire, which is missing in most of the normal people. But we can learn these millionaire qualities and can develop them within us and can become a millionaire.

No1) The very first step is not to take big decisions or to make big plans or team. But the very first step is to DREAM and to have courage and strength to dream big dreams. Sadly, very few able to dream even though it is so easy. You notice by yourself, that most of the people don't even think to dream big. If you talk to them about big dreams, they will either avoid it or else make fun of it. They keep limits for dreams as well. Hence it is the reason they never able to achieve anything big in their life. So do keep this quality of a millionaire in you and start dreaming big.

No2) Self-Employed. Most of the failures do not able to achieve anything big in their life because they always blame or think someone else is responsible for their situation and conditions. Either government, neighbours, relatives etc.

They get somebody to blame and this blaming attitude is the biggest enemy of their dreams. Because if someone thinks that everything which is happening in their life is because of someone else, then due to this attitude that person will never take any action. Because as per them there is nothing in their control and thus, they can't do anything about it. Whereas on the other side, a person who always take responsibility for everything that is happening in their life, starts taking actions, start searching for solutions and no matter how bad situation is, that responsible person will always make the situation better by taking various actions which is the most powerful thing. Trust me Attitude of taking Responsibility has the ability and strength to change the world and becoming a millionaire. Always take responsibility of your life and of your doings.

No3) Work harder and longer. If you work around 40 hours a week, then you are just doing your duty just like many. This only helps you to live an average life. But hours you spend over those 40 hours, those extra hard work and efforts will decide how much successful you'll become. Normal people always want to work 5 days in a week and not more than 8 hours. Whereas on the other side if you see self-made millionaires, they work on an average 59 hours a week. Some even worked for 7o to 80 hours that too without taking any holidays and this hard work paid them very well. Made them a millionaire and bring them to a position where they can take holidays for a month and can go to a world tour that too without any worries. Do remember your success depends on those extra hours and on your hard work. The more you do hard work, the more successful you will become. Never get afraid of going extra miles compares to others. Because in that extra miles you will not get much traffic, will not get much competition. Hence never get afraid of doing more hard work. This will not only make you a respectable person but also increase your chances of becoming a millionaire.

No4) Dedicate yourself to Life Long Learning. Most of the People think that after school or college learning and education ends and then work-life starts and they need to work to earn money. But self-made millionaires understand that the actual learning starts after college life. Hence, they always value lifetime learning. Life-Long Learning is the minimum requirement to become a self-made millionaire. Learning is the most important thing in this fast-changing and growing world. Earlier when people used to have more lands they were counted as rich. Then Industrialisation came, people who had more factories were counted as rich. But Today is Information age, and people who have more information, knowledge has better chances and capabilities to become rich(millionaire). Hence you must have seen mostly self-made millionaires keep on gaining knowledge and information. They listen and read books or they learn through mentors so that their knowledge always increases and can grab the right opportunity at the right time. Give at least an hour or two hours towards learning and gaining knowledge. You can do this through various mediums like reading or listening books or by listening useful podcasts, learning through mentors or by watching various useful videos etc and if you find hard to remove time, then you can take information through audio format, which you can do by doing a lot of other works. For example, an average person wastes most of his time in travelling and in traffic, instead of wasting your time in that traffic you can gain knowledge through audio format this thing will take you ahead compare to normal people and put you under the millionaire category.

No5) Power Of honesty. To create a successful business, trust is the most important and major factor. Because people like to do business or want to help people who are trustworthy and genuine and also buy product or services from such trustworthy and genuine people or company. Your success depends on the number of people who have trust on you. The more the people trust you, the more the chances you have to become successful and the best way to gain that trust is to always be truthful and genuine. Try to keep your integrity and avoiding not to lie no matter what the situation is. This thing will help you for the long term and people will respect you and this thing also gives you lot of opportunities to become a millionaire.

No6) Speed and dependability. In the 21st century, real and new money is time and millionaire, billionaires understand this very well. They always value there's as well as others time. However normal people don't understand the value of time. Millionaires always try to increase the speed of their work, so that they can get more output at lesser time. Whereas normal people waste their time while working and this is the main reason they do not move ahead in life. If someone can finish 1-hour work at 30 mins, everyone will go to that person for their work. This quality can make you successful easily.

No7) Get Around the Right People. 85 per cent of life's happiness and success depends on your quality of relationship which you form with others in your personal and professional life. Meaning the more you know people personally and the more others know you positively, the more chances you will have to move ahead in life. Relations or networking can be very beneficial for you to grow in your life that too in speed. Because in life's every turning point, you can have someone who can help you positively to grow and move ahead in life and the more you have a connection, the more you have chances to get the right person at the right time, who can help you grow.

What daily habits, choices we have to make to get ourselves a success

Keep dreaming always. Never lose on the hope that your idea will be a success and will earn a million dollars.

As an entrepreneur, we all have choices to make in our life. But what life choices, what daily habit, choices we have to make to get ourselves a success. Read this blog below to find out the things we have to do in our daily life to stay in the game.

Our mind is everything. If we will be able to control, able to stable our minds, then we can achieve anything in the world.

- Don't hit snooze on the clock. Wake up early. Wake up at the time you decided to wake up yesterday.

- Keep dreaming always. Never lose on the hope that your idea will be a success and will earn a million dollars.

- Don't worry about what people will think.

- Build a strong team. Bring those people in, who are on the same path as yours.

- Don't waste time on watching movies and series on Netflix. Listen to podcasts. Or watch a shark tank.

- Keep your dream alive to pitch yours's idea to the shark.

- Haters will get you nervous. Treat them as a passing cloud.

- Always keep the dream that one day you're going to be your own boss.

- Don't stay within your limits.

- If you are losing a little money in the process, then don't be ready to call it to quit. Nothing can happen overnight. Success takes time, hard work, dedication, and passion.

- If you really want to stay in the game, then think about why you graduated. You haven't graduated from college for a job. You are an entrepreneur from the start.

- Don't stay dirty like a doormat. Stay fresh like a billionaire.

How some smart people use some dumbest way to get rich?

We all have this idea that you should be smart and work hard to become a millionaire. At the end of the day, lazy people achieve nothing. Fortunately, in the age of capitalism, the rules of the game are quite different and you can get super rich even if you have the dumbest idea possible.

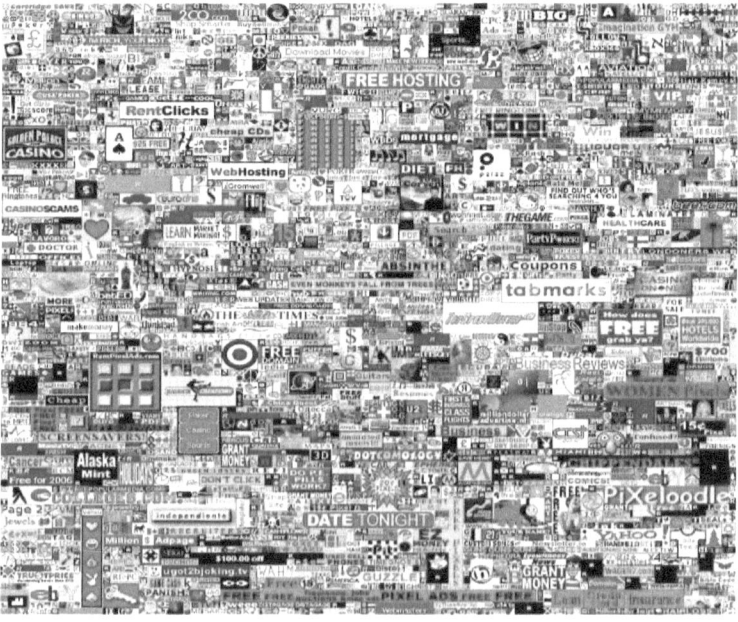

Take an example of Alex Tew who figured out a very creative way to pay back his student debt. At first glance, it seems like this idea is so freaking dumb that it would never work in a million years. Alex realized, making a million-dollar isn't as difficult as it seems. All he needed to do is to sell 1-dollar product to a million people out of 7 billion that are walking on the face of the earth. He created a simple website that consisted of a single page with one million pixels and decided to sell each pixel for a single dollar. Buyers could place their images, logos or ads with an option to add a link to their website. But you can't do anything with 1 pixel. He started selling them 10 X 10, with a minimum price of a hundred bucks. His first customers were his friends and family since he was raising money to pay back his student loan. But after the site made over a thousand dollars, it got the attention of the press who started writing about it and now everyone wanted a piece of the pie. So, within the next month, the website earned over 250 dollars. The battle for the last 1000 pixels were so fierce that they were auctioned on eBay and eventually sold for over 38,100 dollars. The million-dollar Home Page made over a 1,037,100 in 5 months, helping Alex, not only pay back his student debt but make him a millionaire.

What would you say to someone who plans to become a millionaire by winning a lottery! Idiot! right? Because your chances to win a lottery is 1 in 45 million. But that's exactly what Joan Ginther did. She won the lottery in 1993 and earned over 5.4 million dollars and since she has a Stanford Ph.D. in statistics, she did the math and came up with a way to win the lottery again. It sounds like a joke. If it was possible to mathematically win the lottery, everyone would do it. But it seems like she is the only one who could. Since she managed to win the lottery for another 3 times. Her next win came after 13 years in 2006 when she won 2 million dollars. Of course, it's not as big as her first win. So, 2 years later she decided, she needs to match her first prize and won another 3 million dollars. Making her total winnings, 10.4 million dollars. That seems like enough money to retire. However, not for Joan, she decided she needs another 10 million dollars to never worry about her bills again. In 2010, she won another 10 million dollars and it seems like she has retired since we haven't heard about her again. Before we move to our next hero let me just say that I am not encouraging anyone in any way to spend his or her savings on lottery tickets. What Juan Ginther did is truly unique and unbelievable.

However, what you can do is buy a domain for pennies and sell it for millions later on. I am not sure if that's going to work now but that's exactly what Chris Clark did. When he realized that vodka.com was sold for 3 million dollars, he figured out what to do with the domain he has purchased back in 1994 for just 20 bucks. What was another source of a liability, since he was paying the annual fee to keep the domain? Turned Chris into a multi-millionaire overnight! He put the domain up for an auction and sold it for 2.6 million dollars.

The number of people who got super-rich out of ridiculously dumb ideas is way longer than this blog could possibly cover. But you get the picture. If you come across an idea that looks it would never work because it's simply dumb, it might worth giving it a shot. So, no idea or work is dumb. If you are that much dedicated to work it out, then that idea will make you millions.

In the first case, Alex has that marketing skills to make such a dumb idea so viral that he earned so much. In the second case, Joan used mathematics to win the lottery. So, it's really difficult to predict by calculating numbers. But she waited and executed at the right time. In the third case, Chris waited for so many years and paid all the annual fees until one buyer came to buy the domain. He has that much patience to do this.

So, I won't say much. All I want to say is your skill, patience and dedication will get you anything in the world. Never ever lose hope.

Why do start-ups fail?

It's time to get serious. Let's discuss the 3 keys to start-up success bit more in detail.

The first key is your market selection. Last week I was watching "Becoming Warren Buffet" documentary, and I learned the secret of Buffet's colossal success. In that program, Warren shares the story that got him hooked in the early days from a rare book called "One Thousand Ways to Make $1,000." It's the story of "Penny-Weight" Scales Lure Pennies. The idea is to buy a weighing scale, pick a good location, set it up, and it will lure pennies from all those curious to know how much they weigh. It probably worked big time for him. He says, "I had everybody in the country weighing themselves ten times a day and me just sitting there like the John D. Rockefeller of weighing machines." It's a perfect money-making option. All he needs to do was, invest money and put the machine in the right place [or right market] and it'll mint money. Isn't it great? This story and the experience have influenced and shaped Warren's approach from then onwards. If you look at the products and companies Buffett invest in, they all are used by almost everyone. They all are companies that cater to enormous markets like real estate, insurance, jewellery, news media, condiments, and more.

He sells what millions of people want. Because he understood early that the key to success and profits is choosing the right markets, with 80+ billion in net worth, it looks like he is right. And that's where many start-ups fail. 42% of the start-ups fail because of the lack of market need or chose the wrong market. Because in a terrible market, even the best product in the world doesn't matter - you will fail. You'll spend years trying to find customers who don't exist to buy your amazing product, get demoralized, and quit. And your start-up will die.

On the other hand, a great market - a market with lots of real potential customers - the market will produce wonders for the start-up. You don't need to produce an excellent product; you need one that works. And, the market will embrace it, help you build a great one, and make it a huge success. Also, don't worry if the current market size is small. It doesn't matter. What really matters is the market size in 10 years. It is good to be in a small but rapidly growing market instead of a big but stagnated market. Your first job is to identify a good market — a rapidly growing market full of potential customers. Spend as much as the time you need to get this correct and pick a great market.

2020 is here. 12 new chapters and 365 opportunities to do things right, correct your mistakes, go after your dreams, and make your life better. Everything is yours to make it your best year so far. Unfortunately, most people will do exactly what they did last year and the year before that. They will make new resolutions and vow not to make the same mistakes they made earlier. And they will forget them even before the first month is over. The dreams will remain as they are - just dreams. They will take the same actions, get the same results, and when things don't change, they'll have the same excuses and complaints. It'll be the same old ones. They don't have enough time or They don't have the experience or skills or They don't have the money or They don't get enough opportunities or They were planning to do it, but life got in the way and so on. They try to hide everything behind those reasons, stories, and excuses.

In this new year, I've one humble request to you. Whatever you do, please, don't become that person. It's your precious life and dreams. You got to do better than that. Do you know what stops you from doing that? It is not what you lack that is stopping you. It's not your lack of experience or short of skills, or something else is stopping you. What's stopping you is your lack of commitment. You want to change your life, make it better, and make your dreams real. But you are not committed to making it happen. Because when you just want something, it remains a wish. You don't care much about whether it works or not, comes true or not, and if it doesn't work, that's when you come up with stories, reasons, and excuses about why it didn't work. That's how it works "wishes" and "wants." But when you are committed to achieving something, you throw the excuses out and do whatever it takes to achieve the goals and to realize the dreams. You don't wait for the opportunities; you create them. You don't wait for things to happen; you make them happen. And that's when you'll taste success because success favours those who are committed to succeeding. You don't need detailed plans or thorough preparation or anything else all you need to do is to begin, to start. Today.

It doesn't matter how big your dream is or how difficult your goal is, take your first step now, this moment. Most of us forget the power of now. Starting now with whatever, you have is 10X better than starting tomorrow with everything you need because you'll never know what'll happen tomorrow. It's what we do today that decides our future. And you don't need more experience or skills or money or time to achieve things. You already have enough of everything. All you need is to put what you know into action without delaying further or waiting for the perfect moment. Forget what happened in 2019 or 2018 or years before that. Forget everything you've tried. Forget all those excuses. Get rid of all that baggage. They will drag you down. Start fresh today. You've got 365 opportunities to try, to learn, to apply, and to get things right. Let this be the moment you've been waiting for. Let this be your year and make it your best ever. Don't wait for things to change. Go. Make it happen.

www.ingramcontent.com/pod-product-compliance
Lightning Source LLC
Chambersburg PA
CBHW030542220526
45463CB00007B/2941